SPIRIT
SOUL
&
BODY

A Revelation of Man

Romel Duane Moore Sr.

Prayer Changes Things (PCT) Publishing
7551 Kingsport Road
Indianapolis, Indiana 46256

Scripture quotations are from the King James Version of the Bible, unless otherwise noted.

Cover design by Michael Corvin.

No part of this book may be reproduced in any form without permission in writing from the publisher.

Printed in the United States of America.

Edited by Margaret Rose Mejia.

ISBN 9781073342556
Imprint: Independently Published

Copyright © 2019 by Romel Duane Moore Sr.
All rights reserved.

The name satan is intentionally not capitalized.

TABLE OF CONTENTS

Dedication	pg. 4
Introduction	pg. 5
Chapter 1 *Three Branches of Government*	pg. 6
Chapter 2 *Fish, Fowl, and Beast*	pg. 21
Chapter 3 *Servant, Horse, and Prince*	pg. 33
Chapter 4 *The Tabernacle*	pg. 43
Chapter 5 *Peter, James, and John*	pg. 52
Chapter 6 *Jesus' Humanity*	pg. 65
Prayer	pg. 69
About the Author	pg. 70
Footnotes	pg. 71

DEDICATION

This book is dedicated to my co-laborer in Christ, Margaret Rose Mejia. Thank you for your dedication and heart for soul winning.

INTRODUCTION

God created man in His image and after His likeness as a tripartite being who consists of spirit, soul, and body. We are a spirit, who has a soul, and lives in a body. This truth is hidden in biblical types. By using the language of symbolism, the spirit, soul, and body are revealed. It is said that a picture is worth a thousand words. The pictures that Scripture provides help us to unlock the revelation of God's Word. A rich understanding of the makeup of God's highest creation called man, who is a triune being, is brought into greater light with *Redemption's Story* at its heart. We are two-thirds spiritual and one-third natural. It is imperative for every citizen of the Kingdom of Heaven to know how God created us and the Divine order He established for us to live by. Every part of man's triune being has a specific purpose. The focus of this book is to illuminate God's Divine understanding concerning man's unique design of spirit, soul, and body.

1

THREE BRANCHES OF GOVERNMENT

The United States Constitution created the three branches of government: Legislative, Judicial, and Executive.

The Legislative Branch makes the laws and Congress is made up of two entities: the Senate and the House of Representatives.

The Judicial Branch is the Supreme Court and nine Justices make judicial decisions. The Judicial Branch judges the laws that the Legislative Branch passes, based on the Constitution of the United States.

The Executive Branch is the office of the President and his Cabinet. The Executive Branch enforces the laws the Legislative Branch passes.

These three powers better known as the three branches of government can be used as types of man's tripartite being: spirit, soul, and body.

JUDICIAL BRANCH

Let's start with the Judicial Branch of the United States government. The Judicial Branch represents man's soul. It is our soul that judges everything including God's Laws. The soul is the part of man that thinks logically, feels, reasons, uses common sense, intellectualizes, informs, reckons, concludes, solves, surmises, estimates, deduces, considers, concludes, rationalizes, sizes up, calculates, judges, critiques, conceptualizes, believes, and opinionates. From the time we are born in this world, our soul does its job without any real effort. Since we were born spiritually dead and disconnected from God, the soul has received its laws and rules from the fallen nature of the flesh. Therefore, the soul is carnal and in need of salvation. Our soul needs to be redeemed, cleansed, and renewed. Our soul must be reprogrammed and taught the right way to judge. This is done when our soul receives the laws and principles of God after we are Born Again. Hebrews 10:39 says:

But we are not of them who draw back unto perdition; but of them that believe to the saving of the soul.

Our mind, will, and emotions need salvation just as our spirit does. The Born Again experience redeems our spirit. However, the soul is still in need of salvation. God takes care of the spirit's redemption with the new birth, but it is our responsibility to redeem and save the soul. We must willfully and intentionally do what is necessary to cleanse and renew our mind, will, and emotions. It is not automatically cleansed when we give our hearts to Christ. Philippians 2:12 says:

Wherefore, my beloved, as ye have always obeyed, not as in my presence only, but now much more in my absence, work out your own salvation with fear and trembling.

It is the responsibility of each of us to renew our minds and learn the ways, attributes, and Laws of God. If we do not learn the Word of God and submit to the leading and guidance of the Holy Spirit, we will not fully benefit from the Born Again experience. In other words, it will profit us very little in this life from being saved, if we do not save our souls: our mind, will, and emotions. The body does what the mind tells it to do. Obtaining eternal life in the next life will have no true benefit in this life if we do not change how we think and feel. We are only transformed by the renewing of our minds. The mind is our battlefield and it is where we judge everything.

The soul is our Judicial Branch of government and our Constitution is the Word of God. If our "judge" does not know and understand the laws of God, he will unjustly judge the things he sees, hears, feels, touches, and thinks. We recently witnessed one of the greatest fights in American history over the Supreme Court nomination of Judge Brett Kavanaugh by President Donald Trump. The opposition to his nomination was extremely intense because, if confirmed, Judge Kavanaugh would tip the scale of conservative Judges in conservatives' favor. The liberals and Democrats in government were so afraid of this nomination because they feared that all of their ungodly judicial successes could be overturned, like Roe v. Wade and same-sex "marriages." It is our *judge of the soul* who gets the final word and makes the decision if the laws that are passed by the Legislative Branch of the Holy Spirit are valid or not. Like the liberals in government, in America, the devil desires that we keep his judges sitting on the bench of the Supreme Court of our soul.

The devil wants us to continue to judge from an unrenewed soul and strike down the laws and statutes of God as not lawful, in order for us to continue existing in a carnal, defeated lifestyle, void of the principles of the Lord. It does not matter how great America's Constitution is if the Judges who sit on the bench do not interpret its words with the proper meaning of the spirit of the Founding Fathers, who wrote the Constitution. Likewise, it profits the Born Again Believer very little to possess God's Holy Bible if the judge of our soul does not process and filter God's Word from a renewed state of mind. If you pour purified water in a dirty glass, the water will be dirty when an individual drinks it. We are attempting to drink from God's purified Word with unclean souls and it's no wonder we still do not understand His ways and attributes. Our soul is the filter and it must be cleansed.

DECISIONS

The Supreme Court must make a decision regarding every case that is brought before them. The Supreme Court will decide if the case before them lines up with the laws and statutes within the Constitution or if the case is in violation of them. Either way, there must be a decision rendered. It is man's soul that makes the final decision about everything we do. We wake up and our soul decides what we will eat for breakfast, what clothes to wear to work or school, which car to drive to work in, who we will be nice to and who we will ignore. All of our actions and reactions are decided upon by our souls. If our soul isn't renewed by the Word of God and cleansed, it will daily make bad decisions and violate the Laws of God which in turn will cause pain and dis-ease in our lives. As the Judicial Branch of our self-government, the soul is our decision maker.

OPINION

After a case is heard and judged by the Supreme Court, each of the nine justices are required to write an overview of the case. This overview is called "an opinion." It is our soul (our mind, will, and emotions) who renders opinions about everything that happens to us and around us every day. The definition of *opinion* is *a view or judgment formed about something, not necessarily based on fact or knowledge.*[1] From the time we break through the perfect comfort and protection of our mother's womb and give our lungs their first exercise as a healthy cry erupts, we begin to immediately judge everything around us based on our five senses. If we are held, we judge this as love. If we are left alone too long, we judge this as abandonment. We form lightning fast opinions about the most insignificant things around us, as well as the most important episodes in our lives. God created the soul of man to do exactly what it does. However, He wants our soul to function from a place of truth, grace, and wholeness and not from a place of sin, pain, and error. Our soul's job is to judge. However, we have to make sure that the *justices within our soul* judge righteously and not erroneously.

BOOK OF JUDGES

There is a prophetic reason why God chose to include a book in the Old Testament named Judges. After Moses and Joshua were in leadership, Israel transitioned into a period of time where the people were ruled by judges. These were men and women chosen to lead the children of Israel before the Israelites demanded to have a king over them.

And when the Lord raised them up judges, then the Lord was with the judge, and delivered them out of the hand of their enemies all the days of the judge: for it repented the Lord because of their groanings by reason of them that oppressed them and vexed them.

And it came to pass, when the judge was dead, that they returned, and corrupted themselves more than their fathers, in following other gods to serve them, and to bow down unto them; they ceased not from their own doings, nor from their stubborn way.   J
Judges 2:18-19

The Book of Judges serves as a type for man's soul. When Israel had righteous judges, Israel obeyed the Laws of God. Therefore, God blessed them and defeated their enemies. On the other hand, when Israel had unrighteous judges in leadership, these judges caused the people of God to sin before Him. Consequently, the Israelites were then oppressed by their enemies. The Book of Judges reveals what is known as "the cycle of sin." When the *judge of our soul* is unrighteous, we will automatically judge everything around us unjustly. This will undoubtedly cause us to live a life of sin and oppression by continuing in bad habits and harmful addictions. However, when the *judge of our soul* is saved and judges righteously, without fail, our lives will be fruitful, blessed, and free from satanic influences and bondage.

CANAANITE TRIBES

When God appointed righteous judges over Israel, God graced them to help kill and remove the Canaanite tribes out of the land. There were many Canaanite tribes. However, the main six tribes were: the Canaanites, Hittites, Amorites, Perizzites, Hivites, and Jebusites.[2] Every one of these tribes represent an area of our soul that is not renewed, infected with sin, lawless, and wicked. The Promised Land, better known as "The Land of Milk and Honey," was promised as an inheritance to the children of Israel by God. The land was not uninhabited, but had Canaanite tribes dwelling there. Each tribe is symbolic of an area of our mind, will, and emotions that need extraction so the Laws and Principles of God can replace them. The meaning of each Canaanite tribe name gives insight to the different areas of our soul that needs renewing. Canaanite means *one who exists in and for material things; a merchant; a pirate; trafficker in materiality.* There is a part of our soul that is materialistic and desires to traffic in obtaining material possessions. We have to accept the challenge to remove those harmful thoughts, imaginations, and mindsets. Unless the Canaanites are totally removed from your *promised land of the soul,* they will vex you as you attempt to walk out the promises of God in your life. Every city and Canaanite tribe possessing the Promised Land represents a way of thinking, perceiving, and emoting. These thoughts and emotions take up residence in a part of our soul: our mind, will, and emotions. Joshua and the children of Israel removed the Canaanites by killing them with the edge of the sword and the Sword of the Spirit is the Word of God.

UNJUST JUDGE

Jesus spoke a parable affectionately called, *The Unjust Judge.* This parable gives us great insight into the understanding of man's soul as the Judicial Branch of man's self-government. Luke 18:1-8 says:

And he spake a parable unto them to this end, that men ought always to pray, and not to faint.

Saying, There was in a city a judge, which feared not God, neither regarded man:

And there was a widow in that city; and she came unto him, saying, Avenge me of mine adversary.

And he would not for a while: but afterward he said within himself, Though I fear not God, nor regard man;

Yet because this widow troubleth me, I will avenge her, lest by her continual coming she weary me.

And the Lord said, Hear what the unjust judge saith.

And shall not God avenge his own elect, which cry day and night unto him, though he bear long with them?

I tell you that he will avenge them speedily. Nevertheless when the Son of man cometh, shall he find faith on the earth?

Jesus said that this unjust judge did not fear God or regard man. This description of the unjust judge is a picture of man's unrenewed soul. We were born "in sin" and "shapen in iniquity." Therefore, our souls have a sin nature. The soul does not know God and His ways, neither does the soul regard man. The soul is selfish, self-centered, and self-righteous. This story reveals that the only way to get the unjust judge to do what is right is by persistently demanding him to change his mind. The person in the story who accomplished this was a widow woman. In Scripture, the soul is feminine. David wrote in Psalm 34:2, "My soul shall make her boast in the Lord..." We cannot be lazy or procrastinate when it comes to saving the soul. Only the constant bombardment of the Word of God will cause the unrenewed soul to bend to God's will and His ways.

Jesus began the *Parable of the Unjust Judge* by stating, "...men ought always to pray and not to faint." Saving the soul is not a job for the faint of heart. It is a daily task and we cannot be nice about it. It is life or death because "For as he (a man) thinketh in his heart, so is he..." We are the sum total of our thoughts and the Scripture is clear that a carnal mind is death and enmity against God. When we get this revelation we must be consistent and persistent like the woman in Jesus' parable and daily knock on our soul's door demanding it to change. This will take much prayer and unwavering dedication. However, the soul can be made to do, think, and have emotions regarding God's will.

LEGISLATIVE BRANCH

The spirit of man is a type of the Legislative power of government. The Laws of God are made from and by the Holy Spirit. The Word of God is the Sword of the Spirit. Jesus said, "…the words that I speak unto you, they are spirit, and they are life." The Legislative Branch makes the laws and the Laws come from God. It is man's spirit that receives God's Laws. The soul judges the laws that come from the spirit. The flesh (The Executive Branch) enforces the laws that the spirit (The Legislative Branch) receives from God that the soul (The Judicial Branch) judges to be appropriate. God does the work of the Legislative Branch by Himself. The only thing we have to do for the Legislative Branch of the spirit to be saved, is to believe in the work accomplished by Jesus on Calvary. Our Born Again spirit is 100% redeemed and recreated in the image and likeness of God.

The next step is to study God's Word. Then, through meditation and prayer, the Spirit of God will begin to bring illumination and revelation of God's Word. All the laws, statutes, and principles of God come from the spirit. Jesus is the Word of God and all things were made by Him and for Him. He is Creator. Therefore, all laws come from Him and our spirit is the recipient to receive and understand His laws and ways because the spirit is made from the same substance as God. God is a Spirit and they that worship Him must worship Him in spirit and in truth. The more we learn and receive the laws of God, the more ammunition we have to overthrow the unjust judge of the soul. The Word of God is like a hammer breaking the most stubborn stones. The Word of God is quick, and powerful, and sharper than any twoedged sword, piercing even to the dividing asunder of soul and spirit, joints and marrow, and is a discerner of the thoughts and intents of the heart.

EXECUTIVE BRANCH

The Executive power of government is a type of man's flesh. The Executive Branch enforces the laws the Legislative branch makes. Our body will enforce whatever the soul decides upon. The Executive Branch of government isn't supposed to operate independently of the laws the Legislative Branch passes. In like manner, the body does not move independently of the soul. The mind, will, and emotions usually make the decision before the body executes it. If we view man's spirit, soul, and body as a corporation, the spirit is the CEO, the soul is Chairman of the Board, and the body is the company.

Our bodies are supposed to be the Temple of the Holy Ghost. We only get one body and we must take care of it to the best of our ability. This means keeping it free of harmful chemicals and substances, and eating the proper foods in order to maintain a healthy immune system to help ward off diseases. Ultimately, we are to present our bodies as a living sacrifice, holy and acceptable unto God. However, if our soul is not adhering to the Word of God, we are at risk of allowing bad decisions to destroy the only body God has blessed us with. The unjust judge of the soul will decide that experimenting with illicit drugs is okay and spending years in a lifestyle of addiction is proper. An unrenewed soul may believe it is okay to give your body sexually to as many people as possible because it feels good. If you do not save your soul, it is possible to believe you are your own god and do not need to answer to anyone else. You will go about life doing as you please instead of doing the things that please God.

We will be judged by what we do with our bodies: good or evil. God wants us to use our bodies to preach the Gospel of the Kingdom of Heaven to every person and make disciples. The enemy desires to use our bodies in selfish, self-destructive manners that will offend God and cause our days to be shortened. God originally created man in His image and after His likeness and gave man dominion over the Earth. Man disobeyed God by eating from the forbidden tree and experienced a fall. By God's grace, God already had a plan to salvage what was done. This is the basis of salvation through Jesus Christ. God created us as tripartite beings consisting of spirit, soul, and body. We are a spirit, who has a soul, that lives in a body. It is God's will that we use this awesome triune makeup of our spirit, soul, and body to do His will and establish His Kingdom in this fallen world. There is no greater feeling than knowing you are in the center of God's will and your life is honoring the original purpose He created us for: to worship Him and do His will.

2

FISH, FOWL, & BEAST

And God said, Let us make man in our image, after our likeness: and let them have dominion over the fish of the sea, and over the fowl of the air, and over the cattle, and over all the earth, and over every creeping thing that creepeth upon the earth.
Genesis 1:26

In the beginning, God created man in His image and after His likeness and gave him dominion over the Earth. The Scriptures list exactly what man was given authority over. These three categories are the fish of the sea, the fowl of the air, and the beast of the field (and everything that creeps upon the earth). Using the language of symbolism, I will teach you how these three groups (that God gave Adam dominion over) also represent man's self-government. Water is symbolic of the Holy Spirit. Jesus stated in John 7:38-39:

He that believeth on me, as the scripture hath said, out of his belly shall flow rivers of living water.

(But this spake he of the Spirit, which they that believe on him should receive: for the Holy Ghost was not yet given; because Jesus was not yet glorified.)

The fish and living creatures of the sea represent the eternal spirit of man and the Gifts and Fruit of the Holy Spirit. During the Flood, every living creature perished except the creatures who already lived in water. Insects, animals, and birds died, but the living creatures of the sea did not because water was already their habitation. Likewise, man's spirit cannot die. It will live forever: either in the Presence of God or eternally in Hell. The spirit of man was created eternally and it has no expiration date. The fish of the sea is a type of man's spirit. Our spirit is water and the living creatures of the sea are types of the gifts, fruit, power, wisdom, knowledge, and understanding that are inherit in the Born Again Spirit. The oceans contain plankton, plants, algae, marine invertebrates, fish, reptiles, and marine mammals. Living creatures of the ocean range from microscopic to very large mammals. The same is true of the living things inherent in man's Born Again Spirit.

First and foremost, God's Spirit resides within the spirit of man. Upon our new birth, after giving our hearts to Christ, the Spirit of God is the One Who regenerates our spirit and recreates it into the image and likeness of God. Within this recreated spirit is the nature, character, and personality of God. God does not dwell in unclean temples. It is only after our spirits are regenerated in the likeness and image of God that God's Spirit comes to live within the Born Again Spirit that is sinless and recreated in the nature of God. Titus 3:5 states:

Not by works of righteousness which we have done, but according to his mercy he saved us, by the washing of regeneration, and renewing of the Holy Ghost.

1 Peter 1:23 says:

Being born again, not of corruptible seed, but of incorruptible, by the word of God, which liveth and abideth for ever.

John 3:5 says:

Jesus answered, Verily, verily, I say unto thee, Except a man be born of water and of the Spirit, he cannot enter into the kingdom of God.

The fifth chapter of Galatians lists the nine characteristics of the Fruit of the Holy Spirit. Inherit in the Born Again Spirit of man is love, joy, peace, longsuffering, gentleness, goodness, faith, meekness, and temperance. Each of these characteristics are limitless. It is the wet with the water. Smartphones come with certain "apps" (applications) already installed in the phone like Facebook, Twitter, and YouTube. The regenerated spirit comes with the nature and personality of God already installed and the Fruit and Gifts of the Spirit are already in the regenerated spirit's DNA. Many believe the mind of Christ is something we must learn and obtain. However, the truth is we already possess the mind of Christ upon our Born Again experience. Jesus stated in John 14:26:

But the Comforter, which is the Holy Ghost, whom the Father will send in my name, he shall teach you all things, and bring all things to your remembrance, whatsoever I have said unto you.

In Jeremiah 1:5 God informed the Prophet Jeremiah that before he was formed in his mother's womb, God knew him and ordained him to be a prophet. God knew us before we were born physically. There were secret things God spoke to us before we came through our mother's womb. After we are born, we forget all that the Lord spoke to us. However, once we are Born Again, Jesus explains that when the Comforter comes He will teach us and bring all things to our remembrance that the Lord already said to us. He was not only referring to the things that He said to His disciples, but the things He spoke to each of us before we were formed in our mother's womb. When the Holy Spirit gives us revelation, He isn't showing it to us for the first time. He is reminding us or giving us total recall of previous conversations with God that took place before the worlds were formed.

RENEW YOUR MIND

And be not conformed to this world: but be ye transformed by the renewing of your mind, that ye may prove what is that good, and acceptable, and perfect, will of God.
Romans 12:2

We've been taught how the process of renewing of the mind meant to reprogram the mind by replacing old information with new information from the Word of God. Renewing the mind is deeper than this. The only way to renew a magazine subscription is to have first owned a magazine subscription. Renewing the mind isn't limited to learning the Word of God. Ultimately, renewing the mind is connected to Divinely understanding that we have obtained the mind of Christ upon the new birth. Philippians 2:5 states, "Let this mind be in you, which was also in Christ Jesus." Let is a word of permission. We have to let the mind of Christ "come forth" in us. 1 Corinthians 2:16 says, ". . . but we have the mind of Christ."

FOWL OF THE AIR

The second part of creation that Adam and Eve were given authority over was the fowl of the air. The fowl of the air are the birds or the part of creation that flies. They represent the soul of man. The soul is the mind, will, and emotions. It is within man's soul where thoughts and emotions fly. We cannot control every thought and feeling that flies in our mind. However, we can stop them from making a nest. Many of the thoughts and emotions we feel are foul. We were born in this world with a contaminated soul because we were born in sin. We automatically inherited the carnal mind. *Carnal* comes from the word *carnivorous* that means *flesh eater*. Like buying a laptop with viruses already in its hard drive, the soul of man came with the carnal mind operating from the law of sin and death. Saving the spirit of man is the easy part because the Holy Ghost completely regenerates our spirit upon our new birth after giving our hearts to Jesus. The Spirit completely saves the spirit. However, the difficult part and process is the saving of the soul and denying the urges of the flesh. We had no control and get no credit for the regeneration of the spirit. God alone accomplished it through the work of Calvary. The only way our soul is renewed and saved is by our intervention and effort. God does not save our souls for us and He does not bring our flesh under subjection. If we do not do it, it will not be done.

We must understand that until we allow the Word of God to change the way we think and heal our emotions, the things that fly around in our unrenewed soul is foul. The hatred, unforgiveness, greed, anger, pride, lust, and jealousy we feel and think is foul. The carnal cravings of the flesh we allow to roam in our mind, will, and emotions without "checking them" are foul. God gave Adam dominion over the fish of the sea, the fowl of the air, and everything that creeps upon the earth. Jesus restored the original authority and dominion God gave man. Our dominion must begin with and in us before it's relevant anywhere else. If we can't control ourselves, we have no business attempting to control anything else. Paul gave us great insight into our thoughts and how to have dominion over them. 2 Corinthians 10:5 says:

Casting down imaginations, and every high thing that exalteth itself against the knowledge of God, and bringing into captivity every thought to the obedience of Christ.

Paul informed us that our imagination is considered "high." The thoughts flying freely in our minds are "high." They are "high" not because they are holy, but because the mind/head is located at the highest part of the human body. The name of the place the world leaders use to meet was called "a summit" because they met on top of a mountain. The soul is our "summit" and it's where the imaginations and thoughts fly high.

BEAST OF THE FIELD

The third part of creation that God gave Adam authority over was *the beast of the field*. *The beast of the field* is symbolic of *man's flesh*. God told Adam that the day he ate from the Tree of the Knowledge of Good and Evil, he would die. Adam and Eve died spiritually, immediately, as the Spirit of God left man. Adam was created in God's image and after His likeness. However, after he disobeyed God, Adam lost the image and likeness of God and fell into a lower image and nature known as *the image and nature of the beast*. The proof of this transformation is when God came, killed an innocent animal, and clothed Adam and Eve. This was done as the first sacrifice offered to cover man's sins because without the shedding of innocent blood there is no remission of sins. Also, when God clothed Adam and Eve with animal skins, this revealed the new image that man would walk in: *the image of the beast*. When man fell, we fell from the image and nature of God to *the image and nature of the beast*. We lost God's Divine Image and Nature and inherited a lower image and nature, also known as "the carnal man" who possesses the law of sin and death.

There is a "beastly" part of our makeup that must be dealt with. Another description of *the beast of the field* is "everything that creeps." Within our fallen flesh lies the sin nature and "everything that's creepy." Do you know if you walk in the flesh, you are creepy? The flesh cannot be redeemed, saved, or salvaged. The only thing we can do with the flesh is crucify it. Paul explained the flesh in Romans 7:18-21:

For I know that in me (that is, in my flesh,) dwelleth no good thing: for to will is present with me; but how to perform that which is good I find not.

For the good that I would I do not: but the evil which I would not, that I do.

Now if I do that I would not, it is no more I that do it, but sin that dwelleth in me.

I find then a law, that, when I would do good, evil is present with me.

We cannot take "the flesh" lightly. We cannot take chances with this part of our makeup. If we do not kill "the flesh," "the flesh" will kill us. Specifically, "the flesh" will kill our walk with God. The nation of the Amalekites is an example of "the flesh." God instructed King Saul to kill all of the Amalekites. However, King

Saul disobeyed God and saved the Amalekites' king and many of their animals. In the end, since Saul did not kill all of the Amalekites, the same Amalekites killed Saul. There is nothing good, righteous, or wholesome about "the flesh." "The flesh" is the enemy, also known as the "inner me" or "in-a-me." Every human is born spiritually dead, disconnected from God, and has the fallen, sinful, *beastly nature of the flesh*, because of the fall of Adam. Apostle Paul explains it more in Romans 8:1-8:

There is therefore now no condemnation to them which are in Christ Jesus, who walk not after the flesh, but after the Spirit.

For the law of the Spirit of life in Christ Jesus hath made me free from the law of sin and death.

For what the law could not do, in that it was weak through the flesh, God sending his own Son in the likeness of sinful flesh, and for sin, condemned sin in the flesh:

That the righteousness of the law might be fulfilled in us, who walk not after the flesh, but after the Spirit.

For they that are after the flesh do mind the things of the flesh; but they that are after the Spirit the things of the Spirit.

For to be carnally minded is death; but to be spiritually minded is life and peace.

Because the carnal mind is enmity against God: for it is not subject to the law of God, neither indeed can be.

So then they that are in the flesh cannot please God.

The only reason we are able to overcome the desires and works of the flesh is because Christ came and died in the flesh for our sins. He is the Reason we have authority over what the Bible calls: the carnal man, the carnal mind, the old man, and the flesh. These are all synonymous. Paul makes it clear that the flesh cannot understand the things of God and when we walk after the flesh we cannot please God. He went as far as to state that the carnal mind is enmity against God and the carnal mind is death. This means you may be Born Again but if you choose to operate from the carnal mind you are still operating in death because as a man thinks in his heart so is he. We have the right God, the right Book, and the right Laws. However, this means very little if we still think from "the flesh."

"The flesh" is the core of the fallen, sinful nature and it cannot be salvaged. The spirit can be Born Again, re-gened, and recreated. The soul can be saved by the renewing of our minds. However, "the flesh" must die. God has promised every Believer a new body in the resurrection, but this body has no redemption. 1 Corinthians 15:50-57 explains:

Now this I say, brethren, that flesh and blood cannot inherit the kingdom of God; neither doth corruption inherit incorruption.

Behold, I shew you a mystery; We shall not all sleep, but we shall all be changed,

In a moment, in the twinkling of an eye, at the last trump: for the trumpet shall sound, and the dead shall be raised incorruptible, and we shall be changed.

For this corruptible must put on incorruption, and this mortal must put on immortality.

So when this corruptible shall put on incorruption, and this mortal shall put on immortality, then shall be brought to pass the saying that is written, Death is swallowed up in victory.

O death, where is thy sting? O grave, where is thy victory?

The sting of death is sin; and the strength of sin is the law.

But thanks be to God, which giveth us the victory through our Lord Jesus Christ.

3

SERVANTS, HORSES, AND PRINCES

There is an evil which I have seen under the sun, as an error which proceedeth from the ruler:

Folly is set in great dignity, and the rich sit in low place.

I have seen servants upon horses, and princes walking as servants upon the earth.
Ecclesiastes 10:5-7

This proverb from the Book of Ecclesiastes is profound. King Solomon states there is an evil existing and he explains what it is. He did not list murder, rape, or incest. King Solomon said that folly is set in great dignity and the rich sit in low places. The Amplified Version says, "...folly is set in many exalted places and in great dignity while the rich sit in humble places." He goes on to give the essence of what this great evil looks like as he states that he has seen servants upon horses, and princes walking as servants upon the earth. This image gives great insight into the subject matter of this book concerning man's spirit, soul, and body. In this proverb, the prince represents the spirit, the horse represents the soul, and the servant represents the body. The evil that is revealed here is how the spirit, who should be riding the horse, is walking and the servant who should be walking, is riding the horse. According to the wisest king in Scripture, this was evil.

INSIDE OUT

Man is a tripartite being. We are a spirit, who has a soul, and lives in a body. God's original design was for man's spirit to lead through the soul and finally by the body. The fall of man perverted God's original purpose and today we live out the perversion of God's Divine design. Genesis 3:7 explains:

And the eyes of them both were opened, and they knew that they were naked; and they sewed fig leaves together, and made themselves aprons.

Adam and Eve were not blind before the Fall so why does the Scripture state that after they ate from the forbidden tree, their eyes were opened and they knew they were naked? Before the Fall, Adam and Eve were living souls or spiritual beings. Their spirit and soul were seen externally and their body of flesh was hidden internally. Today, our flesh is seen externally, and our spirit and soul is hidden internally inside our body. They did not know they were naked before the Fall because while in their spiritual bodies, they were clothed with God's glory. However, immediately after the Fall, their spiritual eyes were closed (the day they ate they would surely die) and their physical eyes were opened. They saw their physical bodies for the first time because before the Fall their physical body was hidden within the soul and spirit.

Luke 19:10 says, "For the Son of man is come to seek and to save that which was lost." The work of Calvary not only paid the price for man's sins, it also paved the way for man to be restored back to our original design: spirit, soul, and body. Although we may be Born Again and spiritually reconnected to God, we still live in this fallen body of "the flesh" and our regenerated spirit lives inside of our body. We will receive the full restoration and inheritance of God's original intent in the resurrection when we will receive glorified bodies. Solomon revealed that it was evil when servants ride the horse and the prince is walking. This is what happened with the fall of man. Before Adam sinned in Eden, man's spirit (the prince) rode the horse (the soul) and the servant (the body) walked.

HEART OF MAN

For the word of God is quick and powerful, and sharper than any twoedged sword, piercing even to the dividing asunder of soul and spirit, and of the joints and marrow, and is a discerner of the thoughts and intents of the heart.
Hebrews 4:12

This Scripture reveals that the Word of God is the only thing that can divide the soul and spirit. This means the soul and spirit are one before the Word of God divides them. The combination of soul and spirit makes up the heart of man. When we read "the heart of man" in Scripture, it is referring to the team of man's spirit and soul. Adam and Eve were created as living souls. Their external bodies consisted of their spirit and soul (heart). The only thing on earth that can divide the soul and spirit is God's Word that is alive. The soul (mind, will, and emotions) is either the servant to the spirit or the body. We either follow the leadership of our spirit or our body. In the Garden of Eden, Adam's soul served his spirit and his body was hidden and submitted to the leadership of his spirit.

PRINCE

Man's spirit is the prince. The spirit of man is created in the likeness and image of God because God is a Spirit. The Holy Spirit lives in the regenerated spirit of man. The Nature, Character, Personality, Gifts, and Fruit of the Spirit lives within the spirit. God created man's spirit, also known as the "spirit-man," to know God's will. 1Corinthians 2:1-2 says:

For what man knoweth the things of a man, save the spirit of man which is in him? even so the things of God knoweth no man, but the Spirit of God.

Now we have received, not the spirit of the world, but the spirit which is of God; that we might know the things that are freely given to us of God.

First, God's information is supposed to come through the prince of the spirit of man. Second, the soul receives the Divine information and decides, thinks, feels, and wills it. Finally, the body executes God's information. It is a perversion of the Divine design when we allow the body to lead and the spirit to be made subject to the body's urges, desires, plans, and direction. This is what Solomon called evil. God's will never begins with the flesh. The flesh cannot know God's will, or the things of God. Neither can the flesh please God. Remember, flesh and blood cannot inherit the Kingdom of Heaven. God's hierarchy is spirit, soul, and then body. It is not body, soul, and then spirit. Our recreated Born Again spirit is our prince. The prince of our spirit is supposed to ride the horse of our soul.

The spirit of man is so awesome that it has unlimited capabilities as an eternal creation. Moses imparted a portion of his spirit to seventy elders of Israel. This is called "having the spirit of your leader." You literally are able to receive a portion of another person's spirit. In marriage, the husband and wife become one: spirit, soul, and body. Elisha received a double portion of Elijah's spirit. Jesus had the Holy Spirit without measure. God is eternal and our spirit that's regenerated after His image and likeness is eternal like Him. It is imperative that every disciple of Christ learn and understand the power, purpose, and potential of our recreated "spirit-man." The spirit is the prince who should always have leadership of the soul and body.

Our Born Again spirit is our knower. The flesh cannot understand or know the things of God and the soul must be saved by the renewing of the mind by the Word of God. However, the regenerated spirit already knows the will of God and is ready and willing to do His will every second of every day. We spend too much time in our soul trying to comprehend God's will from our emotions, feelings, and mind. The soul needs to calculate, reason, think, rationalize, and emote. On the contrary, the spirit of man knows God's will because he is recreated in God's image and after His likeness. The spirit has the genes of God, the nature of God and knows His ways and attributes. Psalms 46:10 says, "Be still, and know that I am God…" If we wait to connect with our spirit, our "spirit-man" is always still, and he knows the will of God. It is our soul that is always moving and in a rush. The soul is volatile, moody, and at times doubleminded until he is tamed and saved.

HORSE

In Solomon's proverb, the horse represents the soul of man. Any horse that is fit for human use must be broken. Horses are wild by nature and desire to run free. However, before man can properly ride the horse it must go through the stages of being broken of its wild nature and tamed for human enjoyment. The soul is also wild and needs to be tamed in its unregenerate state. From the time we are born in this world, we came here fallen and disconnected from God. We were born with our soul under the sinful leadership of the flesh and operating from the carnal mind. The soul is wild because it operates from carnal desires of the flesh and its mind, will and emotions have run wild without proper restraint and leadership from the spirit and a position of righteousness. Only the Word of God through the leadership of the Holy Ghost can transform the soul and save it. In this aspect, the soul is the horse. However, instead of being ridden by the prince of the recreated spirit, the soul is ridden by the servant of the flesh and Solomon stated that this is evil.

We cannot function without our mind. This makes the soul very important because all the final decisions are made from the soul. Whatever we decide and choose to do, the soul is the part of our triune being that executes it. If our soul isn't tamed, broken, and saved, we are no different than a wild horse that is of no use for human activity. The horse of the soul must be transformed from the leadership of the flesh to the Divine order and leadership of the spirit. If there was nothing wrong with our mind, will, and emotions, the Scriptures would not instruct us to have our minds renewed and transformed. If our way of thinking did not offend God and harm us, He would not demand us to have the mind of Christ. If our emotions were already healthy and wholesome, we would not need emotional healing and the Word of God to assist us in managing our feelings. Before we can get our life in order, we must first get our soul in order. Our actions begin in our minds and we were born with a carnal mind. Salvation serves very little purpose in this life if only our spirits are recreated. However, our souls are never renewed because as a man thinks in his heart so is he. Paul instructs us in 2 Corinthians 10:4-5:

(For the weapons of our warfare are not carnal, but mighty through God to the pulling down of strong holds;)

Casting down imaginations, and every high thing that exalteth itself against the knowledge of God, and bringing into captivity every thought to the obedience of Christ.

THE SERVANT

Our "flesh" has one purpose and that is to serve. Our "flesh" is the servant of the will of God on the earth. The servant should never be in a position of leadership and authority. The fall of man took "the flesh" from a place of obscurity to leadership. "The flesh" cannot be redeemed and is not salvageable. God did not make "the flesh" eternal, the way He made the soul and spirit. Our "flesh" has an expiration date. However, the spirit and soul live forever. This is because we are born in sin and shaped in iniquity with a sin nature. We came into this fallen world in a perpetual state of perversion as the servant of our "flesh" rides the horse of our soul and the prince of the spirit walks. Solomon called this evil because we are born in this world evil, fallen, and disconnected from relationship with God. The Scriptures make this clear that all have sinned and come short of the glory of God. All of our righteousness are as filthy rags. If God was to count iniquity, none of us would stand. In our fallen state, we could not save ourselves. Thank God for sending us Jesus and His gift of salvation. Man can correct the perverted state we came into this world in, only through Christ. Man can leave the evil condition of the servant of our "flesh" riding the horse of our soul, as the prince of our spirit walks, and return to God's original design of the prince of our spirit riding the horse of the soul, as the servant of the flesh walks.

4

THE TABERNACLE

The Tabernacle of Moses is a picture of man's spirit, soul, and body. In the Tabernacle of Moses, there were three sections: the Outer Court, the Inner Court, and the Holiest of All. In order to exit the Outer Court and enter the Inner Court, the priest had to go through a veil that served as a door. Veils have always been used in covenant, intimate settings. Brides are adorned with a veil over their face during the wedding ceremony. The veil is not removed until the very end of the ceremony when the groom is instructed to kiss the bride. At this point, the veil is removed or lifted and intimacy between the two commences through a kiss. True intimacy with God can only be obtained when the veil is lifted. Apostle Paul said that our body is the Temple of the Holy Ghost. Jesus, speaking of His own Body said in John 2:19, "…Destroy this temple, and in three days I will raise it up." **John 2:19** The sides of man's head is called the *temple*. Man's body is his temple and the highest part of the body is the head whose sides are *temples*. Like the Tabernacle of Moses, our temple possesses veils and like Moses' Tabernacle, the veils are where the Cherubim reside. The process of going higher in God is being able to pass through the veil. The Inner Court is smaller than the Outer Court and the Holiest of All is smaller than the Inner Court. Therefore, with each level of our tabernacle, the room gets smaller. Many priests could dwell in the Outer Court. A few could dwell in the Inner Court. However, only one could dwell in the Holiest of All. This is because the closer we get to God, the more focused we have to be. There is no room for scattered thinking and distractions. This type of ministry is considered sacred and we must begin to understand that the condition of our minds is very sacred to God. As the mind goes, the body goes. God speaks to all of His people, whether leaders or lay persons, through the *cherubim* (imagination) of their minds and hearts. Intimacy with God is through our *cherubim*. Numbers 7:89 says:

And when Moses was gone into the tabernacle of the congregation to speak with him, then <u>he heard the voice of one speaking unto him</u> from off the mercy seat that was upon the ark of testimony, <u>from between the two cherubims</u>: and he spake unto him.

Exodus 25:22 says:

And there I will meet with thee, and <u>I will commune with thee</u> from above the mercy seat, from <u>between the two cherubims</u> which *are upon the ark of the testimony, of all things which I will give thee in commandment unto the children of Israel.*

WHERE GOD DWELLS

Our mind possesses our *cherubim* (imagination) and this is what makes us living creatures. God does not live in buildings made from wood and stone. We put too much attention and detail into the physical houses where we worship. However, the only house God ever intended man to worship in is within his heart. The building of temples, tabernacles, and churches are all results of the Fall of man. Genesis 3:8 says, "And they heard the voice of the Lord God walking in the garden in the cool of the day . . ." The first question we must ask is how can a voice walk? God's Voice is His Word and Jesus is the Word of God. Therefore, this was another way of saying that Jesus came walking in the garden. The Voice of God, Who was walking, came looking for Adam and Eve (who were now fallen) and asked the question, "Adam where are you?" Why was God's Voice asking about Adam's whereabouts? Adam housed the Voice of God because God created Adam in His image and after His likeness. God breathed into Adam His very own Breath. This is how Adam was able to rule and reign on the Earth because God's Voice lived inside of him. When Adam spoke, creation heard God's Voice. Immediately, after the Fall, Adam lost God's Voice and now the Voice of God came looking for Adam asking his whereabouts because the only place God ever desired to dwell was inside of man.

Today, we are more concerned with the beautification of buildings made with hands, instead of the beauty of the true temples of God, who is man. God is not impressed with our great cathedrals and magnificent edifices. The best marble, ivory, gold, and silver will never be a sufficient substitute for the heart and soul of man. God's first indwelling of man was by His Breath (wind). Then, after the price was paid for man's sins, He was ready to live inside man again. It was culminated on the Day of Pentecost when the Holy Spirit came into the Upper Room like "a rushing mighty wind." The end result was that 120 Believers began to speak in new tongues. When God lived inside of Adam, Adam possessed God's Voice and when God lived inside of the first Believers on the Day of Pentecost, His Voice lived inside of them and the evidence was new tongues.

GOLDEN CHERUBIM

The highest level of the cherubim of our imagination is when it becomes a part of the Ark of the Covenant. The third section of the Tabernacle was a small room called the Holiest of All. The Holiest of All was where the Shekinah Glory of God dwelt and the only furniture in this room was the Ark of the Covenant. In Old Testament times, the Presence of the Ark represented the very Presence of God. Israel did nothing important as a nation without the Ark going before them, first. The Ark went first during the crossing of the Jordan River into the Promised Land. It went first as Israel marched around the walls of Jericho. It was a symbol of God going before them and giving them victory. The Ark consisted of one large piece of pure gold beaten into the form of two large cherubim (winged angelic beings) facing each other, whose wings overshadowed the Mercy Seat in the middle of the two cherubim. Our advancement mentally and imaginatively into God's Holiest of All is the highest achievement of any man. The two cherubim and Mercy Seat were all beaten from one large piece of gold because it represented the man's mind becoming one with God and when this happens, man's mind will be connected to the mercy of God. The Mercy Seat was golden because mercy is a Divine attribute. The ability and desire to forgive someone only comes from God. Man is at his best when his mind is golden, connected to God's Mercy Seat. Many who call themselves Christians do not display this characteristic. However, anyone who says they are a Child of God will undoubtedly be seated in mercy toward their fellow brother. The only way we can prove our love for God is by how we love our neighbor. Apostle John said, "If a man say, I love God, and hateth his brother, he is a liar:

for he that loveth not his brother whom he hath seen, how can he love God whom he hath not seen?" 1John 4:20 We cannot. So the proof of our love for an invisible God can only be revealed by the love we have for one another. When the cherubim of our minds become golden, it will no doubt be one with mercy. The honor of having our thoughts and imagination changed from carnal, lustful, and "normal" into golden and glorified is nothing less than miraculous. This is supposed to be every human's greatest goal in life: to have the mind of Christ. To think like Him, feel like Him, emote like Him, and reason like Him is to have reached the highest goal. Adam's mind was golden (Divine) because He was made in God's image and after God's likeness. Adam's mind and emotions were golden because God breathed His own breath into Adam and made him a living soul. Adam's mind was golden because God gave him the ability to be fruitful, multiply, replenish, subdue, and have dominion over the Earth. Adam's mind was golden because he existed in Eden, a place of voluptuousness and delight. This is where Christ came to restore us back to: The Place of the Skull!

MERCY SEAT

On the Day of Atonement, the High Priest first sprinkled himself with the blood from the sacrificial lamb, then he was instructed to enter behind the veil into the Holiest of All with blood to sprinkle on the Ark of the Covenant. This included the golden cherubim and the Mercy Seat. Hebrews 9:22b says, "...and without shedding of blood is no remission (of sins)." Isaiah 37:16 says, "...God of Israel, that dwellest between the cherubims." God's Glory filled the Holiest of All and He spoke from the Ark. The entire structure of the Tabernacle of Moses is a picture of the makeup of man. Man is spirit, soul, and body and the Tabernacle had three separate sections consisting of The Outer Court, The Inner Court, and The Holiest of All. Everyone could see into The Outer Court where sacrifices and death took place. This represents the body of man because everyone can see our body. The human body ages and will eventually die. The Inner Court consisted of a Table of Shewbread with Golden Candlesticks and the Altar of Incense. The Inner Court was hidden behind the first veil and it's the soul of man that is hidden behind the veil of flesh. It's our soul that contains our mind, will, and emotions. The soul of man is our Table of Shewbread. It is where we are fed the Word of God and our mind, will, and emotions dwell here. The priest had to light the Golden Candles daily in the Inner Court. This means the light in the Inner Court was not purely Divine. Man had part of the responsibility to keep the candles burning. It is the soul of man that is spiritual and hidden behind the veil of flesh. The Candlelight of Illumination burns within the soul. However, if we do not change the wick and add the fire of God's Spirit on a daily basis, it can grow dark and dim. The soul is where we find intercession because the Altar of Incense is located here. We pray, stand in the gap, intercede, and offer up to God our supplications through the soul. It produces a sweet smell and ascends to Heaven on our behalf. The third level of the Tabernacle is the Holiest of All and this is a type of man's spirit. Only one person was allowed behind the veil into the Holiest of All. And only one Person is allowed into the spirit of man and that is the High Priest Jesus Christ, Who shed His own Blood for the regeneration of our spirits so that communion with God may be restored. The Holiest of All contained one piece of furniture and it was the Ark of the Covenant. The spirit of man was created to house the Ark of the Covenant which represents God's Presence. There is hidden Manna in our spirit. The Commandments of God are written in our spirit. There is a rod that buds with the fruit of healing and deliverance inside the Born Again spirit of man. God is a Spirit and when we are Born Again He makes His abode in our spirit because of the shed Blood of our High Priest Jesus Christ.

We must understand that God is seated in Mercy. *Mercy Seat* is literally translated *seat of grace*.[5] The evidence that God dwells inside man is the grace and mercy we display to those who are around us. God is not seen in great Scripture quotes or religious activity. Jesus said that the number one attribute to know who His disciples are, would be the love they have for one another. If we call ourselves Believers in Christ and have no outward evidence of unconditional love, mercy, and grace toward our neighbor, we are liars and hypocrites. These attributes are only developed when our cherubim are transformed into golden cherubim and God feels welcome again, to dwell between them. Are we seated in grace and mercy? Or are we seated in the seat of the scornful? This was where Adam was originally seated (in grace and mercy) and it is where Jesus redeemed us back to sit again.

5

PETER, JAMES, & JOHN

And after six days Jesus taketh Peter, James, and John his brother, and bringeth them up into an high mountain apart.
Matthew 17:1

Jesus had twelve disciples. However, Peter, James, and John were His closest three disciples. On many occasions, Jesus separated these three disciples so that they could see and hear certain things. I believe one of the reasons Jesus gave them special attention was because they represent man's triune being of spirit, soul, and body. Jesus' personal interactions with these three disciples will reveal symbolically how this is true.

JOHN, THE BELOVED

John was the youngest of the twelve disciples. Most Bible scholars believe John was a teenager around the age of sixteen. John represents the spirit of man because he was affectionately called "the beloved disciple" and it is our spirit that is beloved of God because God lives within our spirit. He was the compassionate and affectionate disciple. John 13:23 says:

Now there was leaning on Jesus' bosom one of his disciples, whom Jesus loved.

John wrote the Book of John and is referring to himself in this verse. As he often laid on Jesus' Breast, it could be assumed he not only openly showed his love for God's Presence on Earth, but was probably fascinated with Jesus' heartbeat. In other words, John was close to God's heart and was in tune with His heart. This is indicative of how John represented the spirit because it's the recreated spirit of man that is made in the likeness and image of God and only desires to do what's on the Father's Heart. The spirit has God's DNA and loves what the Father loves. Our Born Again spirit only yearns to lay in the Bosom of Jesus. The spirit is one hundred percent redeemed and loves to do the Lord's will. The spirit always wants to pray, worship, give, meditate, love, be patient, show compassion, and forgive. Like John, the spirit is the one whom Jesus loved.

Jesus saith unto him, If I will that he tarry till I come, what is that to thee? follow thou me. John 21:22

After Jesus' Resurrection, Peter was still disputing with Jesus about John. Jesus stated something very prophetic when He stated to Peter that if He chose for John to live until His Second Coming, it was not Peter's business. Jesus wasn't only setting Peter straight concerning Jesus' business with John, but I believe He understood John's role as a type of the spirit of man. He was giving us inside information about the spirit being eternal. It is not coincidence that out of all the disciples, John lived the longest and was not murdered like the other Apostles, but died an old man.

The Revelation of Jesus Christ, which God gave unto him, to shew unto his servants things which must shortly come to pass; and he sent and signified it by his angel unto his servant John. Revelation 1:1

It was not by happenstance that John would live the longest and would be the apostle blessed to receive the Revelation of Jesus while banished to the Isle of Patmos. The part of our triune being that receives revelation is the spirit of man. God is a Spirit and when He speaks to us by His Spirit, it is directly to our spirit. When Jesus asked His disciples, "Whom do men say that I the Son of man am?", Peter responded that Jesus was the Christ, the Son of the living God. Jesus replied to Peter, "flesh and blood hath not revealed it unto thee, but my Father which is in heaven." This affirms that revelation only comes from God. There is nothing God would desire to do more than fellowship with us and when He does, it is Spirit to spirit. The first area of our being that is redeemed is our spirit and it is because God is a Spirit. He saved us spiritually so that He could commune with us as often as we desired. We use our mouth to talk to God and our mind and emotions appreciate and feel Him. However, our first place of contact with God is with our spirit. What we say to God with our mouth is communicated by our spirit. John is a picture of the spirit of man because he was the disciple laying on the Lord's Bosom and the one whom Jesus loved.

When Jesus therefore saw his mother, and the disciple standing by, whom he loved, he saith unto his mother, Woman, behold thy son! John 19:26

After they realized their Lord would be crucified, all of Jesus' disciples (except John) abandoned Him out of fear. John was the only disciple who never left Jesus. John was the only disciple who attended the Lord's murder. He never left Jesus' side! Likewise, our spirit loves the Lord and will never leave Him. We may abandon our relationship with God mentally and physically. However, if we are truly Born Again, our recreated spirit will never deny Him. Even when we are in outright rebellion, our spirit who is created in His image and likeness continues to yearn for us to repent and humble ourselves before God.

GOD'S LOVE

John was described as the disciple whom Jesus loved and as a result he became the disciple of love. The Gospel of John reveals the attribute of Christ's undying love for man. John also wrote the books of 1st, 2nd, and 3rd John. All three books admonish the Believer to walk in the love of God. 1 John 3:18 says:

My little children, let us not love in word, neither in tongue; but in deed and in truth.

Love was the number one characteristic of being a citizen of the Kingdom that John wanted us to understand and activate in our lives. John 3:16 says, "For God so loved the world, that he gave his only begotten Son, that whosoever believeth in him should not perish, but have everlasting life." It penetrated John's heart when he heard Jesus state, "By this shall all men know that ye are my disciples, if ye have love one to another." John heard Jesus state that all the commandments hang on these two: to love God with all your heart, mind, and strength and to love your neighbor as yourself. John understood that salvation came through Christ for one reason, because He loved us and the only proof of our relationship with God is how we love humanity. If we do not have love, we do not have anything! This attribute of John, the love of God, is also indicative of the Born Again spirit. God is love and His followers will not be distinguished by their gifts, oratory skills, charisma, or spirituality, but simply by our love. The spirit of man is full of the love of God and when we walk in the Spirit, we are walking in God's unconditional love. John is the disciple whom Jesus loved.

PETER, THE CONVERTED

And the Lord said, Simon, Simon, behold, Satan hath desired to have you, that he may sift you as wheat:

But I have prayed for thee, that thy faith fail not: and when thou art converted, strengthen thy brethren. Luke 22:31-32

Peter is one of Jesus' three closest disciples who represents the soul. The soul is spiritual like the spirit. However, it is unlike the spirit because the soul is not redeemed. God left our souls' salvation up to us because the soul is our mind, will, and emotions. God will not make us think, feel, and will a certain way. God left that up to us as moral agents whom He has given free will. 1 Peter 1:9 says, "Receiving the end of your faith, even the salvation of your souls." The spirit received its salvation immediately when we gave our hearts to Christ. However, the soul is saved through the process of renewing the mind and allowing the Teacher and Comforter of the Holy Ghost to lead, guide, and teach us according to the Word of God. The beginning of our faith was the salvation of our spirit and it was recreated after God. The end of our faith will be the salvation of our souls, our mind, will, and emotions.

Peter is a type of the soul because he was double-minded, emotional, and always had an opinion. Our soul must be renewed and made to line up with the leading of the Holy Spirit, the Word of God, and His will. One day Peter is in tune with the will and mind of God and the next day Peter is in direct opposition to God's will and mind. One day Jesus asked, "Who do men say that I am?" Peter responded correctly by telling Him that He is the Christ, the Son of the Living God. Jesus informed Peter that flesh and blood did not reveal that to Peter, but the Father in Heaven. Shortly after, Jesus informed the disciples that He will be crucified and rise on the third day. Peter responded by telling Jesus that he wouldn't let anyone touch Him. Jesus rebuked Peter with these words in Matthew 16:23:

But he turned, and said unto Peter, Get thee behind me, satan: thou art an offence unto me: for thou savourest not the things that be of God, but those that be of men.

On one occasion, Jesus complimented Peter by telling him that God spoke through him. However, later on, Jesus rebuked Peter and informed him that satan was speaking through him. This is an excellent picture of man's soul. The soul must be transformed, renewed, reprogrammed, and saved. The soul doesn't like to sit still. It must be moving, thinking, emoting, rationalizing, calculating, opinionating, feeling, judging, etc. It must be taught and tamed to line up with the will of God that comes through the spirit. Like Peter, our soul has days where it lines up with the mind of God and submits to His will. Then, we have days where our soul is in rebellion and agreeing with the works of the devil. This is why Jesus told Peter that the devil desired to have him and sift him as wheat. Jesus went on to say that He prayed for Peter and instructed Peter that after he was converted, he was to strengthen his brethren. Like Peter, the soul must be converted. Conversion is a process and saving the soul is also a process. The devil understands that as the head goes, so does the body because as a man thinks in his heart so is he. We are the sum total of our thoughts. If the enemy has our mind, he has our life, even if we are Born Again, because a carnal mind is enmity against God and the carnal mind is death.

CHICKEN

When Peter rebuked Jesus by telling Him that he would never let anyone crucify Him, Jesus prophesied to Peter that Peter would deny Him three times before the cock crowed. After Jesus was arrested by the High Priest is soldiers, Peter and the other disciples were recognized by a woman and accused of being with Jesus. With profanity, Peter began to deny knowing Jesus and immediately after Peter's third denial of Christ, the cock crowed. Peter saw Jesus from afar and looked directly into His eyes. This of course broke Peter to his core and he ran away. The significance of the cock crowing after Peter's third denial of Christ is that the cock typified who Peter was in his unconverted state: a chicken. The cock is the head, male chicken in the henhouse, but still a chicken. The cock walks around making a lot of noise, pecking all the other chickens, and bullying them. However, in the end he is still a chicken. He is loud, and cocky. Nevertheless, no matter what he does, he is still a chicken.

That life lesson informed Peter that out of all his bodacious talk, in the end, he proved to be nothing more than a loud-mouthed chicken. On many occasions Peter was cocky around all the other disciples, especially John. It all came to a head as Peter was humiliated in their presence and ran off like the chicken he was. Peter's plight is a picture of the soul. Our soul has a lot to say with its multi-dimensional complex makeup. However, in the end, the soul is a chicken in its unregenerate state and will deny Christ under pressure. The soul must be saved, converted, and tamed. The soul cannot save itself. It came into the world in a perverted state of being led by the fallen flesh. Like Peter, the soul must go through the rigorous process of being converted. It will not be easy. Like Peter, there will be humiliating times. However, in the end, the soul can be saved and led just like God created it to do. The only way we can be transformed is by the renewing of the mind. If we do not do our due diligence in renewing our mind, our soul will continue in its doubleminded state and in the end, our soul will cause us to deny the Lord. Peter was converted and in the end, he died by being crucified upside down. Jesus prophesied Peter's death in the same conversation when He told Peter that He could keep John alive until His Second Coming. Jesus' death in the flesh was by crucifixion. Peter insisted on being crucified upside down because He did not feel worthy to die the same way Jesus died.

JAMES

James was one of Jesus' three closest disciples. However, less was written about him than Peter and John. James was the brother of John and on one occasion, he and John asked to sit on Jesus' right and left hand. This was prophetic because as John represents the spirit, James represents the flesh. The right side represents the side of blessing and the left side represents the side of curses. This is seen in *The Story of the Goat and Sheep Nations* in Matthew Chapter 25. James represents the flesh, not because he was evil, but because he was the first disciple to die and also because of how he died. The spirit and soul are spiritual and cannot die. The flesh is the only part of our tripartite being that is physical, cannot be redeemed, and must die. Out of the three disciples who represent man's spirit, soul and body, James was the first to die. Likewise, our flesh must be the first to die after our conversion since flesh and blood cannot inherit the Kingdom of Heaven.

Now about that time Herod the king stretched forth his hands to vex certain of the church.

And he killed James the brother of John with the sword. Acts 12:1-2

James was murdered by the sword. As a picture of the flesh, the way we kill the flesh is with the Sword of the Spirit, which is the Word of God. James wasn't murdered by some random person. King Herod had him murdered. Jesus is the King of Kings and the Lord of Lords. As our King, it is Jesus who demands the death of the flesh immediately after we are Born Again. The King demands the death of the flesh by the Sword of the Spirit. Under the leadership of Joshua, the inhabitants of Canaan were killed and removed by the sword. The only way "the carnal six nations" that dwell within the flesh will be removed from our Promised Land is by the ministry of the Sword of the Spirit, that is the Word of God. The Word should not be used by itself, but only through the Leadership and Power of the Holy Spirit. If the Holy Spirit is not moving, God is not talking. The letter kills, but it's the Spirit that gives life.

We have to sit under the ministry of the Word of God for a long time. Then we will be able strong enough to handle circumcision. Under the law of God, the circumcision of a newborn male child was to be performed on the eighth day of his birth. Medical science recently discovered that the eighth day in the life of a male boy is exactly when the child has enough vitamin B and clotting ability to sustain a circumcision without any assistance. God knew this when He made man. However, man took six thousand years to figure out that God knew what He was talking about long ago. The eight day old male child did not circumcise himself and God does not require any Babe in Christ to circumcise himself either. The priest was required to cut the newborn and the ministry of the Apostle, Prophet, Evangelist, Pastor and Teacher in your life will be the one skilled in the use of the Sword of the Spirit to cut the flesh away in our lives. James represents the flesh and he was killed by King Herod. The flesh in your life has a death sentence assigned to him by Jesus Christ our King because He knows if we do not kill the flesh, the flesh will kill us. We have been Born Again into the Kingdom of Heaven. However, flesh and blood cannot inherit the Kingdom, so the flesh must die.

6

JESUS' HUMANITY

Jesus is one hundred percent God and one hundred percent man: The God-Man. He was so much man that He wept at Lazarus' grave and so much God that He raised him from the dead, after Lazarus was dead for four days. Jesus was so much man that He cried "I thirst," from the Cross. However, He was so much God that He wasn't killed but Jesus "gave up the ghost." Jesus was so much man that He was born in a manger and so much God that He got out of the grave. He is the Last Adam and the Son of Man. Jesus had a spirit, soul, and body. This is unequivocally proven by His experience in the Garden of Gethsemane. Matthew 26:38 says:

Then saith he unto them, My soul is exceeding sorrowful, even unto death: tarry ye here, and watch with me.

This passage reveals how Jesus' soul was in great agony, even to the point where He felt like He was dying. The reality of going to the crucifixion was moments away and

His humanity was agonizing over the pain and torture that He was about to endure for our sins. Jesus requested that His closest disciples, Peter, James, and John pray with him during this troubling time. However, they fell asleep. Just four verses later, the Scriptures reveal this:

Watch and pray, that ye enter not into temptation: the spirit indeed is willing, but the flesh is weak. Matthew 26:41

After the Scripture explains to us how Jesus' soul was exceeding sorrowful, it later reveals from Jesus' own Words that His Spirit was willing, but His flesh was weak. This proves that Jesus had a spirit, soul, and body. Many believe man is a dichotomy, consisting of only soul and body. However, the Scripture is clear we are spirit, soul, and body. 1 Thessalonians 5:23 says:

And the very God of peace sanctify you wholly; and I pray God your whole spirit and soul and body be preserved blameless unto the coming of our Lord Jesus Christ.

THREE GARDENS

God always does things in threes: Abraham, Isaac, and Jacob; Outer Court, Inner Court, and the Holiest of All; thirty, sixty, and one hundred-fold; and good, acceptable, and perfect will of God. God told Adam that the day he ate from the forbidden tree, he would surely die. This death was threefold because man is a tripartite being, consisting of spirit, soul, and body. Adam died spiritually, instantly after he ate, as he was spiritually disconnected from God. Adam inherited the carnal mind (that is death), as his soul slowly died. Finally, Adam died physically. Since man fell in a garden, when God was ready to redeem man, He did it in three stages and He did it in three gardens.

First, in the Garden of Gethsemane, Jesus' soul was in great agony unto death. When He sweat great drops of Blood, He was redeeming the soul of man. Second, as Jesus hung from the Cross, the thief on His right side said, *"...remember me when thou comest into thy kingdom."* Jesus' response to Him was, *"Today shalt thou be with me in paradise."* **Luke 23:42-43** "Paradise" was the Garden of Eden. The Garden of Eden had been translated to the middle part of the Earth, also called "Abraham's Bosom" or "Hades." He died and went to the original Garden of Eden called "Paradise" to perform what the Bible says, *"...he led captivity captive, and gave gifts unto men."*

Ephesians 4:8 This completed the *Redemption of Man* spiritually.

Third, the tomb that Jesus was buried in, belonged to the rich man Joseph of Arimathea and this tomb was in a garden. This is why on Resurrection Sunday, Mary Magdalene thought Jesus was the gardener. ***John 20:15*** Today, the place where Jesus' tomb is located is called *The Garden Tomb*. God placed the first Adam in the Garden of Eden and told him to keep it. On Resurrection Sunday, the Second Adam was mistaken for a gardener. When God resurrected Jesus from the dead, the Bible says that the graves of the Saints were also opened and the Saints of old walked in Jerusalem. ***Matthew 27:52-53*** When Jesus stepped out of the tomb and into a garden, it completed the *Redemption of Man* and the promise that one day we would receive glorified bodies. Man fell in a garden, and man was redeemed in three gardens. We have complete redemption, spirit, soul and body!

Prayer of Salvation

Heavenly Father, I come to you admitting that I am a sinner. I choose to turn away from sin, and I ask You to cleanse me of all unrighteousness. I believe your Son Jesus, died so that I may be forgiven of my sins and made righteous through faith in Him. I call upon the Name of Jesus Christ to be my Savior and the Lord of my life. Jesus, I choose to follow You and I ask that You fill me with the power of the Holy Spirit. I declare I am a child of God. I am free from sin and full of the righteousness of God. I am saved. In Jesus' Name. **Amen.**

About the Author

Romel Duane Moore Sr. passionately preaches the Word of God without compromise and has a unique way of motivating the Body of Christ to evangelism, "good works," and outreach ministry. In January 2019, Pastor Romel established Kingdom Convoy, a "Church without walls," in Hawaii. He believes that we are the Church and brings the Church door-to-door, to the homeless, to teens in juvenile facilities, and to the incarcerated. Pastor Romel is a "prolific writer" and has published 22 books and counting. His books contain exceptional revelations and bring fresh insight from the Word, provoking the reader to "study to show himself approved unto God." All of Pastor Romel's books are available on Amazon and Kindle under the author's full name: Romel Duane Moore Sr.

SPIRIT, SOUL & BODY

Footnotes

[1] The definition of *opinion* is *a view or judgment formed about something, not necessarily based on fact or knowledge;* OxfordDictionaries.com; Copyright © 2019 by Oxford University Press; https://en.oxforddictionaries.com/definition/opinion; Accessed on 6/05/19.

[2] *Judges 3:5* And the children of Israel dwelt among the Canaanites, Hittites, and Amorites, and Perizzites, and Hivites, and Jebusites.

[3] *Caananite*, ca'-naan-lte (Hebrew)--*one who exists in and for material things; a merchant; a pirate; trafficker in materiality.* Truth Unity; Copyright © 2019 by TruthUnity Ministries; https://www.truthunity.net/mbd/canaanite Accessed on 6/06/19.

[4] The definition of *carnivorous* is *flesh-eater;* Dictionary.com Unabridged based on the Random House Unabridged Dictionary; Random House, Inc. Copyright © 2019; https://www.dictionary.com/browse/carnivorous ; Accessed on 6/06/19.

[5] *Mercy Seat* #3727 *kapporeth* in Hebrew means *propitiatory.* The New Strong's Expanded Exhaustive Concordance of the Bible, Copyright © 2010 by Thomas Nelson Publishers. Published in Nashville, TN, by Thomas Nelson, Inc.

Mercy Seat #2435 *hilasterion* in Greek is a neutral of a derivative of #2433; an *expiatory* (place or thing), for example (concretely) an atoning victim, or (specifically) the lid of the Ark (in the Temple):- mercy seat, propitiation. The New Strong's Expanded Exhaustive Concordance of the Bible,

Copyright © 2010 by Thomas Nelson Publishers. Published in Nashville, TN, by Thomas Nelson, Inc.

#2433 *hilaskomai* mid. voice from the same as #2436; to *conciliate*, for example (transitively) to *atone* for (sin), or (intransitively) be *propitious*: - be merciful, make reconciliation for. The New Strong's Expanded Exhaustive Concordance of the Bible, Copyright © 2010 by Thomas Nelson Publishers. Published in Nashville, TN, by Thomas Nelson, Inc.

#2436 *hileos* perhaps from the alternative form of 138: *cheerful* (as *attractive*), for example *propitious*; adverb (by Hebraism) **God be gracious!**, for example (in averting some calamity) *far* be it:- be it far, merciful. The New Strong's Expanded Exhaustive Concordance of the Bible, Copyright © 2010 by Thomas Nelson Publishers. Published in Nashville, TN, by Thomas Nelson, Inc.

Made in the USA
Columbia, SC
04 May 2025